Happy Valentine's Day

Happy Valentine's Day

Published by Stratford Living Publishing.

ISBN Print: 978-1-990332-36-4

Happy Valentine's Day

Dedicated to you.

Happy Valentine's Day

Valentine's Day Will Be Here Soon

And everyone will start getting mushy

Kissing and hugging and all that stuff

Sure makes me feel yucky!

But Mommy and Daddy understand

And so they decided to...

Include me every single year

Because Valentine's Day is for kids too!

For breakfast Daddy makes heart shaped pancakes

He calls them his Valentine's Day art.

Mommy makes heart shaped sandwiches for lunch

After school we play games
- everyone takes part.

And pretty soon it will be time to...

Jump Jump Jump and Say Valentine's Day is for kids too!

In class we watch Gnomeo and Juliet

Some kids make kissing sounds - how rude!

After dinner we will watch The Princess Bride

And when there's kissing I'll know what to do

Cover my eyes -
Jump Jump Jump and Say...

Valentine's Day is for kids too!

Some kids say Valentine's Day isn't much fun

They think it's yucky
to say I Love You

But remember it's only one day of the year

And if that doesn't help you know what to do...

Jump Jump Jump
and Say

Valentine's Day is
for kids too!

And a
Happy Valentine's Day
To You!

Other books in the
Jump Series:
Jump Like a Caribou!
Jump Like a Kangaroo!
Jump at the Zoo!
Jump and Say P.U.!
Jump and Say Boo!
+ New Books Soon!
Other Children's Books:
Billy Shakespeare
Billie Shakespeare
The Three Boulders